SQL Programming

The Ultimate Step-By-Step Guide to Learning SQL for

Beginners

Table of Contents

Introduction

Congratulations on purchasing *SQL Programming,* and thank you for doing so.

The following chapters will discuss everything that you need to know when you want to start implementing SQL and its databases into your business model. There is often a lot of information that a business needs to keep track of, from their customer information to their product information, and having an effective database to hold onto this information can make a big difference in the success that you will see. There are a few different databases that you can choose to work with, but the SQL language and database associated with it is becoming the industry standard overall.

There are a lot of different things that we are able to learn when it comes to the SQL language. To start, we are going to look at some of the basics that come with SQL. We will look at what this language is all about and why it has gained so much popularity in recent years. From there, we will move on to some of the basic commands that work with SQL, the different types of data that are recognized in this language, and some of the methods that you can use to manage this data.

Once we have spent some time handling the various objects that show up in these databases, we will talk about how to do a few of your own search results to find what you need and even how to work with relational database concepts. From there we will spend some time learning how to define some of the data that we want to use with the SQL language and can help us to make sure everything goes in the right place as we code.

The end of this guidebook is going to help us to explore a few important topics that come with using the SQL language. We will look at how to do a few important tasks like working with queries, views, and indexing, and then move on to keeping the database secure since it could potentially hold onto a lot of personal information, and your customers and other users expect you as a business to keep that information safe and away from the wrong hands. We will spend the last part of this book looking at some real-world situations when you can use the topics in this guidebook to get the results that you want with SQL.

As you can see, there are a lot of different options and topics that we need to explore when it comes to working with the SQL database and language. There may be other kinds of databases out there that you are able to work with, but none are going to work as well and provide you with the results that you want for your business. When you are ready to learn more about the SQL code and how to make it work, check out this guidebook to help you get started!

Books about the subject flood the market and we thank you for choosing this one! Please Enjoy!

Chapter 1: The Basics of SQL

If you are looking at learning one of the new coding languages that are available, you may notice that there are a lot of options out there that can be great to work with. Some of these are going to be designed with the beginner programmer in mind to make things easier. Some of these languages are going to be better to use with more advanced coders, work better with one kind of operating system over another, or will help with designing things like websites.

Another option that you can make when choosing a coding language to work with is SQL. This is a great coding language that can be used by businesses to make sure they stay properly organized and are able to keep track of customer and business information while avoiding some of the challenges that come with this as well.

Traditionally, it was common for many companies to work with what was known as the DBMS, or the Database Management System, to help them to keep this information organized, and to make sure they could keep track of their products and their customers. This was one of the very first options on the market for this kind of organization, and you will find that there are many things to enjoy about this system.

While DBMS is going to work well for helping you get some of the work done that you need to with databases, you will find that through the years, there are also a few newer methods that have been released that have changed the way companies will hold onto and sort their information. Even with some of the most basic systems for managing your data, you will see that there is more security and power in these versions than there was in the past.

Many larger companies are responsible for holding onto a lot of data, including some information that is personal about their customers. Information like names, address, and credit card information could be a goldmine if it isn't stored properly, and a hacker or someone else was able to get ahold of it. And as technology grows, it is important for businesses to be able to properly manage these systems and keep things in check and working well. Due to that the information that these companies need to hold is going to be more complex than ever before, the Relational Database Management System has been created in order to keep the information safe, much safer than the DBMS system was able to do in the past.

Now, if you are a business owner and need to keep track of valuable information about customers in your system, you will have a few choices in what you want to get out of a good database management system. While there are a few different options, the one that most companies will like to work with is the SQL. SQL language is one of the best options for doing this work, it is one of the easiest to work with, and was designed to work well with some businesses and will give you all of the tools that you need to make sure that all of your information is safe and sound.

There are a lot of reasons why you would want to protect the information of your customers. Not only will this help to keep your customers safe, but it ensures that your customers still have faith and trust in your business. The SQL language will be able to help you make sure this happens. Let us take a look at the SQL language and learn how to make this work well for your own business.

The SQL language is going to be unique compared to some of the other coding languages that you are able to use. It is going to work in a slightly different manner than some of the others. It is designed for you to be able to work with a database and create a lot of indices and tables that will work for your own needs.

Many companies are going to rely on these tables and databases to help them run. You can use them to help you keep your business employees in order and hold onto their information. You can have a database that helps to hold onto the work that each employee is doing and provides them with roles and access depending on the work that they do. You can even work with a database that helps you to keep track of customer information and some of the products that you are offering.

Let's look at a quick example. If you have a store that sells a variety of products, and you allow your customers to use a search box to type in the item that they want to look for, then you have worked with a database that may be working with SQL.

When the customer types in the term that they want to find, the SQL language is set up in a way that it is able to take that query and look through the database. If everything has been set up in the proper manner, then you will be able to get the right kinds of search results to show up in the next window. This helps the customer to find what they are looking for, without them having to go through your whole database to find the right product. This may not seem like a big deal if you have ten items for sale, but if you have 10,000 items, it can really make the process more efficient and the customer happier.

This is just one of the examples of what we are going to learn how to do with the SQL language. This language is so much easier than you may think it will be when you first get started. As we go through this guidebook, we will look at a few examples of the coding that you will need to do with this one, and you will be surprised at how easy it is and how much more you can do.

If you have ever worked with any other coding language in the past, or even taken a look at how they work, you may be a bit scared by all of the work and the complicated codes. But with SQL, you can use just one or two words on most of the codes, and then the database will do what you want. Let's dive into this and see a bit more about what you can do to see the results you want with your SQL database.

What is the SQL language?

The first thing to take a look at here before we do any coding is what the SQL language is all about. SQL is going to be a type of programming language that you can work with that stands for Structured Query Language. This language is pretty simple to learn because it helps you to interact with the different types of databases that you add to the same system. It also helps a company to keep track of the information that they have for their customers and for their products.

This database system first was released in the 1970s, but when IBM came out with its own type of programming language, we saw SQL really start to grow in popularity. It didn't take long before a lot of companies started to take notice and wanted to use this system.

The version of SQL that IBM was using went under the name of ORACLE. In fact, this became such a successful piece of technology that it wasn't long before there was a split and ORACLE left IBM and started out as its own company. ORACLE, due to some of the ways that it is able to work with SQL, is still one of the programming language leaders in the world, and it is easy to see some of the ways that this program is keeping up with changes in the database management and programming world.

ORACLE®

The SQL language is going to be like a set of instructions that you can use to help you have some interactions with your relational database. While there are going to be other coding languages that you can bring in to get this kind of work done, SQL is the only language that most databases used by companies will be able to understand.

This can make life easier when you already know how to use SQL and how to make it work for you. Any time that you want to interact with many of the databases out there, you will be able to use the SQL software to go in and translate any of the commands that you are given, whether you do this through some mouse clicks or with the use of form entries. These will then be turned over to SQL statements that the database is ready to interpret pretty easily.

As we go through this, you will find that this process has three main components, and we are going to discuss these in more depth later in this guidebook. But the three main ones that you will most likely work with include Data Definition Language, Data Control Language, and Data Manipulation Language.

If you have had a chance to work with other software programs that are driven by databases, then it is likely that some form of SQL has been used in it as well. It is likely that you were able to use the SQL program without even knowing that you were using it. For example, if you are working with a dynamic web page that has a database to drive, it will have forms inside. And if the forms are filled out and clicked on to get to the database, then the information is composed into an SQL query. The query is then able to go through and get the information, or store the information, with the database and do the action that is needed.

Let us take a look at how this is going to work. If you are on a website looking through an online catalog for something, you will want to keep on searching until you find an item that you want. The search page that you use will often contain a form with a simple text box. If you don't want to go through and look at every page for that catalog, you will need to type in the search query, and it will take a look at and bring up the results.

The SQL in this part is going to use the information that you typed in and look through the database to see what it can find that matches up with the search term that you used. As soon as you do click on the search button, the webserver, with the help of SQL, will be able to go through and see if the database will find anything related to that search term. It can then bring back the items that match on a new web page and hopefully, if it is working well and the items have been stored in the proper manner, you will be able to find the things that you want through the database.

For those who haven't been able to work with a learning programming language, and who haven't done any coding, you may find that the commands that are needed to make the SQL language work will not be that hard. Commands that are present in SQL are all designed with a syntax that fits in with the English language.

You will be able to start with a command statement that you will use to describe the action you wish the program to take. From there you will have a clause that follows this and that helps describe the target of the command. This could include something like a specific table in the database that is affected by the command. And to finish this off, there is going to be a series of clauses that are responsible for providing the information that is needed.

While this may seem like a lot of steps to keep track of for a beginner, it is just a few steps, and then you will have a command done that tells the database what you need to pull out. Often you may find that just by reading out the SQL statement, it is going to help you to figure out what you can get the command to do. A good example of how the code can work is below:

DELETE

FROM students

WHERE graduation_year = 2014

Read out the code above, and you can get a good idea of what is going to happen when you decide to execute it. Most of the codes that are presented in this program are going to work in a similar manner to this, which means it is easy for us to figure out how to write the codes that you would like. It won't take long to be able to read through the codes, make sure that everything is in place, and to do the actions that you would like.

If you have never been able to work with any kind of programming language in the past, then you will likely feel a bit worried about working with this and how to get it all set up for yourself. But we are going to explore a bit more about what you can do with this language, and the control that you can use over any database that relies on SQL as well.

Using SQL to work with your database

If you do decide that the SQL language is the right one for you to use when it is time to manage your database, then we need to go back through and look at the database a bit. As you are looking at this notice how the database is just going to contain groups of information. Some people may call these a kind of organizational mechanism that is used to store information that you can go back and look at later on. It can do this as effectively as possible. And SQL will make sure that you have all of the tools that you need to effectively manage any database that you want.

There are going to be some times when you work with some kind of project, and you are working on a database that shares many similarities to SQL. And you may have already been doing this in the past without realizing what was going on. For example, one database that you may have used at some point is a phone book. It may not be the traditional database that we consider, but you will find that it includes the name of a person, their address, their phone number, and even their business if you are in the yellow pages. And all of it is in one place like databases are supposed to be making it easier to find the information that you want quickly and effectively.

This is similar to the way that an SQL database is going to work as well. This language can find the information that you want by looking through the information that is available on any database that you give to it. It can then sort through that information so that you have the best chance of finding the information that you want, without a bunch of searchers and without adding in a lot of time in the process.

Relationship databases

With that in mind, we need to jump in and look at some of the different things that you can do with databases and SQL, and some of the other information that is going to help us get a good start. First, we need to look at the relational database. This is the database that you will work with when you have a database that is aggregated into tables or logical units, and then you want to be able to have the ability to connect the inside of your database, in a manner that makes the most sense for what is asked for at that time.

This is a lot to think of at this time. This kind of database is going to be a good option to use if you would like to take a look at information that is complex. Then, when that information has been looked over, you want to get the program to break down the information into some smaller pieces so that it is easier for you to manage the whole thing.

There are different times when you will want to work with the relational database. This is because they will allow you to take up all of the information that a particular business has stored, and then you can manipulate the information in a way that makes it easier to use, and even easier to read through and learn about in the long run.

You can use the relational database to take some of the complex information that you have available, and then break that up into smaller pieces where others can see what is going on and what is going to work the best for you. To make this a bit easier, this kind of system can go through a database and all of the information inside of it and then will make sure that the information is sorted and ready to go in no time at all.

It is also possible to go through this process and add in a bit more security. Meaning that if you do need to add in some customer personal information at one point, it will ensure that this information is kept as safe as possible, especially when it comes to those who would want to take the information and use it for their own personal gain.

The client and server technology

In the past, if you were trying to do some computer work for your business, you were likely working with a mainframe computer. What this means is that the machine you were using would hold onto the large system, and then this system would be the part that would store all of the information that was needed to do the processing. The user would be able to get onto the computer when needed and interact back with the mainframe, which would be known as a dumb terminal because it is not able to interact all on its own.

Now, if it were true that the user wanted to be able to get the information to show up with the correct function that they need, then the terminal would need to be able to rely on the information that is found inside of the computer, including the storage, the processor, and the memory.

At this point, you may see that the traditional manner may work well, and wonder why we would need to change anything up at all. They were able to get the job done for a company for a long time which made them very popular and, likely, some companies would not want to change it out at all. If you are already using this kind of system and you don't want to pay to get an upgrade, then it is going to do the work good enough. But with the help of SQL, there are a lot of options out there that are more popular and easier to use, and these are going to be found with a system known as the client-server system.

When we are looking at the client-server system, you will see that the system is going to use a different process to get the results that you would like. The main computer in this one is going to be known as the server, and it is technically available to anyone who is considered on the network.

Not just anyone can get on the server though. The user who tries needs to have the right kind of credentials before they are allowed because this adds to a level of security and safety to the process. But if the user comes to the network with the right information, and is found to be a part of the network, they will be able to gather the right information that they need in no time.

The user can get to the server from any other computer that they are using, and in this case, they will be known as the client for this process. This helps to make sure that both the client and the server, or the user and the main computer, can interact with each other with the help of this kind of database to get it done.

Working with the online database

As a business owner, you may find that the client and server technology that we just talked about is going to be the one that works the best for you. This system is great in many cases, but there are going to be some things that you will have to take away or add at times because of all the changes that have been happening to it later. Because of this, some companies are moving their databases online because this opens up some freedom and ensures that the database is going to work with any client, no matter where that client is located.

If you have ever signed up for an account with a company and had to come up with your own username and password, then you have likely worked with one of these databases in the past. As the trend continues for more companies to move their work online, it is going to be more common, and many of the databases that are in use today are going to be moved online as well.

Before a company decides to do this though, it is important for them to take the time to add in some extra security, especially when compared to some of the databases that they may have used in the past. There are hackers and others with ill-intentions who would love to collect the valuable information from places like Amazon, and security is of utmost importance to protect the customers if you do decide to move the database online.

Some of the reasons that SQL is so beneficial!

Now that we have a better idea when it comes to what SQL is all about and why some companies are going to want to use this to work with their own databases, it is time to look a bit more at some of the benefits that come with this language. There may be some other database languages that help you do the same thing, and there are certainly a lot of programming languages that can be adapted to do the work as well. Why is SQL so special, and why would you want to use it for your own needs?

There are several benefits that come with using the SQL language to deal with some of the databases that you have, and some of the best benefits are going to include:

1. Incredibly fast: If you would like to work with a type of management system that can work with the information quickly, and it is possible to get the results back that you need in no time, then the SQL language is a great option to go with. It only takes a few searches using this language to see just how responsive and quick it can be.

2. Standards that are well defined. The database that works with the SQL language is one that has been working well for a long period of time. It also has some great standards that will make sure the database is strong and will work out the way that you would like. There may be other databases out there that are similar, but their standards are lower, and this can make your work a bit frustrating.

3. There isn't a ton of coding. Yes, SQL is known as a programming language. But you don't have to learn lines and lines of coding in order to make this work. As we go through this guidebook, you will notice that there are a lot of codes we practice, and they don't require a ton of work either.

4. Keeps the database organized. When you are trying to run your business, it is important that you can keep the information secure and safe, as much as possible. And while other databases strive to do this, they are not going to help you get all of this security done like SQL can for you.

5. Object-oriented DBMS: The database that comes with SQL is going to rely on the DBMS system that we talked about earlier. The reason that it does this is that this all makes it easier to find any of the information that you need, stores the right items at the right time, and can make it easier to do the other actions that you need in this database.

Above is just a few of the different benefits that you can get when you decide to work with this language. While some people find that the interface of SQL is going to be different than what they have worked with in the past, it is something easy to work with, and before long, you will find that if you are working with a database of any kind, then the SQL language is the best one to get started with.

Chapter 2: Basic Commands That Work Well in SQL

Now that we have had a bit of time to learn more about the SQL language and how this kind of language works, along with some information about databases and how SQL works with these databases, it is time to get to work! Now we are going to look a bit more at the SQL system and look at some of the different commands that you will need to use to make sure the SQL system is going to do the exact actions and searches that you would like.

While it may sound like we are just jumping right into this and can seem a bit scary, don't worry. SQL is one of the easiest languages for you to learn how to use, and the codes are some of the easiest to write out of all the other coding languages. This will ensure that those who are beginners can work with this language as well.

To help us out with some of the commands that you need to learn how to use in SQL, we are going to need to split each of them into six different categories. Each of these categories is important to do some of the code that we want, but doing this will make it easier to understand how each one works with the others and with the program. The six categories of SQL language that you can work with includes:

Data definition language

The first category that we need to take a look at is going to be known as the data definition language or DDL<. It is one of the aspects that are in charge of allowing you to generate some new items into a pre-existing database before you go through and arrange these new objects in the way that makes the most sense for your needs.

For example, this is going to be the part of this system that you will want to use any time that you need to make any change to the table of your database. So, if you want to add in a new object or delete an object, the DDL is going to help. There are a few different commands that are going to fit into this category and they include:

1. Drop index

2. Alter an index

3. Drop view

4. Create an index

5. Alter a table

6. Drop a table

7. Create a table

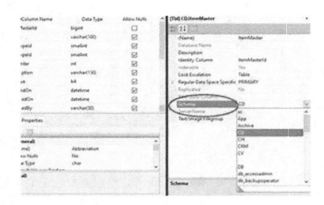

Data manipulation language

The second category that we can put our commands into will be the data manipulation language or the DML. This is going to be the part of the system that you are able to use when you would like to take some of the objects that are in your database and then try to modify them. This is going to make it easier because you and the user have some freedom when doing a search of the information found in the database, and can sometimes free up some more room so that you can add in information that is newer or more relevant at that time.

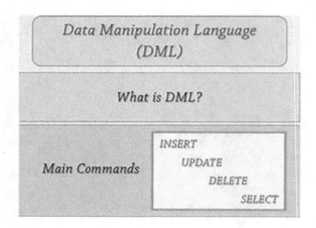

Data control language

On to the next category for your commands in SQL. This is the category that you are going to use any time that you need to add in a bit of power to the codes that you decide to write when you are writing codes. This one will work the best when you want to have a bit more control over how many people, or who can get access to the database that you have made.

If your company is making a database that may have a lot of personal information about the customer, including their names, their address and their credit card information, it is best if you can work with this data control language. This is going to give you the ability to place limits on who can use the database and who can access the information. Some of the things to remember when you decide to work with the data control language include that the DCL command is going to be used to help generate any objects that you need to help you have control over who accesses the information in the database.

There are times when you need to have a bit of control over who can get onto and look at the information in a database, and who has to be kept out. The data control language is going to make this happen. Some of the things that you are able to do with this kind of command will be getting control over those who get onto the database, who can distribute any of the information that is on it, and so much more.

There are a few different commands that you are able to work with when it comes to the data control language commands, and some of these include:

1. Create synonym
2. Grand
3. Alter password
4. Revoke

Data administration commands

As you work with some of the different commands that show up in the system, you will also find that there are some that are able to audit and analyze the operation that is found in the database. There may also be times where you would like to access how the database is performing with the database overall, as long as you use the right commands to make it happen.

If you are working on one of your databases, and you would like to be able to fix something that is not necessarily working the way that you would like inside of the database, or you feel that there are a few bugs in the system that you want to be able to take care of and remove from the system, then the data administration commands are going to help to make this happens. Some of the commands that you are able to use that fit into this include:

1. Start audit
2. Stop audit

One of the things that we have to remember when we use this, and when we are working with the SQL system is that the data administrator and the database administrator are going to be two different things. So, the database administrator is going to be the person in the coding that is able to manage all the aspects that come with the database, including some of the commands, and has the total control for doing this.

Transactional control commands

There are going to be times when you will need to manage, as well as keep track of, a lot of transactions that happen in the database. If you are trying to do some of these actions in the database, you will need to work with what is known as the transactional control commands to make this work. If you are a company that plans to use their own website to help sell some products, then the transactional control commands are going to help make sure everything stays organized. There are a few things that you are able to use this kind of command for including the following:

1. Commit: This is going to be the type of command that you will use when you would like to save some information that relates to the various transactions that show up in the database.

2. Savepoint: this is another command that you will use when it is time to generate two or more points in a group of transactions. You can also use it along with the rollback command to get more done.

3. Rollback: This is the command that you are able to use when it is time to take a look through your database, and you are trying to see which thing you are able to undo inside of your database.

4. Set transactions: With this command, you will be able to use it any time that you would like to provide a name to the transactions that you can find in the database. The set transaction is going to make it easier to label the things that you would like to end up with more organization in the system overall.

As you can see here, there are a lot of different things that you are able to do when it comes to the commands in the SQL language. They are going to make sure that you get the most possible out of the searches and can help the database to provide you with any information that is needed. We will look at some more about these codes and these commands as we go through, but having some basics down and understanding how the system works can make a big difference in the kind of results that you will see.

Chapter 3: Are There Different Types of Data to Use in SQL?

Now that we have had some time to look at the different commands that come with SQL, it is time to take a look at some of the data types that need to come with the process as well when you are creating new code. These types of data are going to change on occasion, based on the action that you would like to complete on your own inside the database. It can also depend on the products that you want to offer to and even sell to the customers.

	postgresql	sqlite	sqlserver	sybase
:binary	bytea	blob	image	image
:boolean	boolean	boolean	bit	bit
:date	date	date	date	datetime
:datetime	timestamp	datetime	datetime	datetime
:decimal	decimal	decimal	decimal	decimal
:float	float	float	float(8)	float(8)
:integer	integer	integer	int	int
:string	(note 1)	varchar(255)	varchar(255)	varchar(255)
:text	text	text	text	text
:time	time	datetime	time	time
:timestamp	timestamp	datetime	datetime	timestamp

The different types of data that you are likely to find in this kind of system will be the attributes that can go with the information that is on the inside, and then you can use these characteristics to get things placed on the table. When the characteristics are in the table, you are able to read them, fix them, modify them, and retrieve them any time that you need.

To help us get a better understanding of how this is going to work and why the SQL data types are important here, we need to look at an example. You are working on a program or a database, and you want to make sure that one particular field is going to be able to hold nothing except numeric values. You can use the SQL system to set this up to ensure that if the user tries to put in letters, that the table will make an error or they are not able to type up anything at all and they can just type in numbers. This could be done when you want the person to just write in their phone number, their credit card number, or their zip code.

With this idea, if you have a cell on your database table that needs to just have numbers on it, such as the phone number, then you would need to add in this kind of restriction to the code. By assigning the right data types to the fields that are going to show up in the table, you can solve some problems ahead of time and can make sure that the customer will see fewer errors in the long term.

One thing that we need to remember with this one is that when you work with this system, all of the versions are going to be slightly different, and the way that you do this process, and some of the choices that you are able to make with it are going to change up as well. You need to check out the rules that come with the SQL version that you plan to work with to make sure that it is going to work the way that you would like.

To help us work with the types of data in this system, it is important for you to know the basic types ahead of time. No matter which version of SQL you are working with, there are going to be three types of data that show up in each part, and these include:

1. Character strings
2. Tie and date values
3. Numeric strings

The character strings

The first thing that we are going to take a look at when it comes to data types in SQL is the character strings. We need to take a look at the fixed-length characters first. If you plan to work with some constant characters or even some strings that you want to make sure stay the same all of the time, you have to take the right steps, and use the right restrictions, to make sure that they get saved inside of your system in the right manner. The data type that is going to work the best for this to ensure that you pick out characters in the proper manner includes the following sample:

CHARACTER (n)

Take a look at the example below, and notice that there is an 'n' that we are able to place in the code above. This one is going to be important because it is going to be the assigned length, and sometimes the maximum length, that you are going to allow to show up in a particular field.

Let's say that you choose to use this as a phone number field. You would want to set the n at 10 because that is as many numbers as you want to allow inside of that part of the table. This is just one example of how you could work with when it comes to limiting your characters. This works fine if you want to have the user put in the phone number or zip code, for example. But if you put this into something like the name part, you will end up cutting some people out of the mix because their name is longer than the maximum that you had put into the code.

Depending on what kind of version that you have with SQL, you can find that you will need to work with the CHAR data type rather than the CHARACTER that we did before to set up the fixed-length that you are going to work with. It is often a good idea for you to work with this data type if you want the information that the user adds in to be alphanumeric.

So with this one, you would end up placing the name of their state, but you want to make sure that they are using the abbreviation, such as NE rather than Nebraska, rather than the whole name of the state in this process. You would be able to use the character limit to just two here so that the other person can figure out what they need to do here.

When the data type of character comes up, your user is not going to add in information that is longer than the character limit you set. If the phone number is needed, you will need to set it at ten. If you want to limit the length of the state, you would put it at two characters. It will all be dependent on the kind of forms that you want to use, and the information that is going to become a part of your set of data as you do things.

The variable characters

Now that we have a good idea what the character strings are going to be, it is time to move on to the second thing that you can fix here. This is going to be the variable characters. It is possible that you are able to work with the variable characters rather than the fixed length characters that we had in the last sections. Rather than only allowing the user to go with so many characters, you can also ask the user to pick out how long this whole thing should be.

This is something that you will want to do in situations like when the user needs to write out their name, including the usernames and the passwords, and more. This allows the user to put in their full name, and then they get the choice of making the username and their password as unique as they will need. To make this notation work in the SQL code, you will need to use the following code to help.

CHARACTER VARYING (n)

Using the code that we have above, you are going to see that the n is going to be the number that you are able to use in order to identify the maximum or the assigned value. You will then need to go through and pick out a form there more than one kind of option that you would like to put in there to help with the characters. Some of the options that you are able to choose here in terms of the variable characters include ANSI, VARCHAR, and VARCHAR2.

For the type of data that we are working with here, there is not going to be any requirement that you have to meet for filling out space. The user is not going to be limited here, which can be nice in many situations. If you did go through and add in a limit of 15 characters, this one would allow the user to write out an answer that is anywhere up to 15 characters. They could also do less than 15 if that is what they want, and it would go through as well.

Any time that you would like to do a few character strings that are going to be more variable, such as a name rather than something like a state abbreviation, you will want to work with the various characters. The reason for working on this is because it allows for us to maximize the space that you are able to use in your database and it can help the user to put in the information in the correct manner, without any errors or confusion showing up in the database in the process.

Numeric value

In addition to working with the two options for characters that we talked about before in terms of the length of the variables that you do, you will also be able to work with the numeric values and how you are able to use it in the SQL language. It is possible to add in values that are numeric at any point that it makes sense with your code. You won't want to add in numbers during the name point of course, but in other options, you will be able to do it for other parts as needed in the code.

These values are going to be the ones that you are able to store right in the field with the use of a number, without needing to add a character if the user doesn't want to. These values are going to come in with a few different names based on which numeric value you would like to use in the code. However, there are some that are more common to work with, and the options that you can include in your code includes:

1. Decimal
2. Real
3. Bit
4. Float
5. Integer

6. Double precision

7. Bit varying(n)

Literal strings

The next option that we need to take a look at here is going to be the literal strings. These are going to consist of a series of characters, and the length of these will be as long or as short as you need. It could be the name and the phone number that will be specified by either the database or the user based on what you are trying to do at the time. For the most part, these strings will be able to hold onto a ton of data, as long as the data held into it is going to be characteristics that go with it.

Now, if you do decide to work with some of these literal strings, you may find that you can run into trouble when it is time to specify the data type you would like to work with. When this happens, you may need to spend some time specifying the type of string that you want to use so that you can double-check that it is going to work the way that you would like. It is good to understand that when you do this, especially if you are working on a string that includes letters and numbers, you need to have some quotes that go around the world to make it work better. You can pick either to use double or single quotes, as long as you use them the same on both sides.

Working with the Boolean values

In many cases, you are going to get into the Boolean values when you work in SQL because they help you do many functions in this system, and they will make it easier to complete the searchers that you or your user will want to do in the database. There are three options that come with the Boolean values, and we are going to take a look at each of them. The three options that come with the Boolean values are going to include true, false, and null.

As you write out some codes that have Boolean values, you may find that using these will be helpful when you are trying to compare more than one data in the table at the same time. You would be able to use these units together with the Boolean value to compare whether the two or more parts are the same or not. This is a good way to set up some of the parameters that come with the search, and when things are compared together and seen as similar, then those would be the results that show up for you.

With the Boolean values, it is important to remember that it is only going to give you some results when an answer comes back as true. If the answer to these values is either false or null, the data is not going to be taken out of the database at this time. If the answer is going to be true, then this is what will show up on the screen when you are done with the query.

A good way to explore this a bit more is when the user is trying to utilize the database and you are trying to find something that is inside a large amount of information. If you are searching for a product, for example, the Boolean values would be able to help you here. If the keywords of the product match up with the query that you are doing, then the ones that match will come up on the screen, and the others will not join the list.

If you are a business with your own website and you are trying to sell a few things online, you may find that it is common for you to use these Boolean values, which is why we are spending some time exploring this topic now. These values are going to be responsible for making sure that when a query is done on your website by a user, the right results that match up with that query will show up on the computer.

There are going to be a lot of different applications where you are able to use the Boolean expressions inside of this language, but as someone who is just learning how to work with this language, this is probably the way that you would use the Boolean expressions the most. You can also use it any time that you have your own personal database, and you can find some answers to a question that you have, or when you are looking through the store or program, and you are trying to get things to match up.

Whether you are looking for using these Boolean values to help you to create a website that finds the results that someone is looking for when they search through your products, or you are using it to go through your own database to find the information that you need, the Boolean values are going to be there to help you get this done. They work on the idea of the answers being true, false or null, so if the products are set up in the database in the proper manner, you will find that you should get the right products to match up with the queries users submit when you use the idea of the Boolean expressions.

As you can see with the different topics we have discussed in this chapter, there are a lot of different types of data that you are able to work with when you choose the SQL language. Using these different types of data in the right place will help to make searches easier, and will ensure that your program is going to work the right way each time.

Chapter 4: Managing Objects in SQL

This guidebook has taken a bit of time for us to look over the different topics and the types of data that is important for this kind of language, it is time to take a look at some of the methods that you are able to use to help manage objects. There are a lot of different techniques that you are able to use when it comes to managing some of your objects in SQL, so let's get started!

Looking at the schema

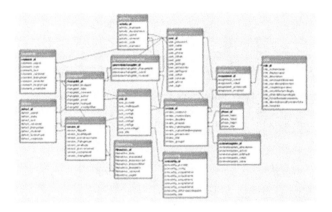

The first topic that we are going to talk about in this chapter is known as a schema. With these schema's, you will think of it as using a set of objects that you can already find in the database, but which need to be linked back to one user, rather than to all of the users, who are on that database. This means that just one user is going to be able to access the schema and see the objects that are inside of it.

Think of this like having your own account on a website. The user may be able to use some of their personal information like address, username, credit card information, and more, along with some of their purchases in the past. This is information that only the user would be able to access with the use of their username and password, and other users on that same database, unless they had this information, would not be able to access the account.

The objects that are on that part of the database, or for the account, are going to be linked directly back to whatever username the owner decided to pick out. The user will then have the power to generate objects, and when this is all done, it is time for them to finish the process to generate a brand new schema. This is a neat thing because it ensures that the user is able to control what is found in their own personal database, and they can make the changes to that database that they see fit.

You will find that there are several ways that this is going to be helpful. In one instance, the user may be in need of placing an order with a company. If the user already has their own account, which would consist of their own schema, they would be able to make and place the order, and then they would be able to delete or change the order if they choose. They can even go through and delete an order or change it when they need to.

Often this is going to be shown when the user goes and tries to set up their own account in a store of yours. This is something that they can optionally decide to do or something that you as the business require them to do in order to make the purchase. This allows them to have an account in the store and they can pick out the password and the username that they want to have associated back with the account, ensuring that there is some level of security that goes with it.

Once your new user has been able to set up the account that they want to use with your website, they will have access to any of the database that actually pertains to them. They can look up their orders, and what they have saved, they can look at the items and products for sale and more. But they will be a bit restricted because, for example, they will not be able to take a look at things like what orders another customer, in particular, has placed.

Now it is time to take a closer look at how this is going to work through an example. You want to set up some credentials for any user who wants to get onto the database, the credentials that they have to meet in order actually to use the sight. If they don't have the right credentials, then the security you set up will make sure they are not allowed on the system at all.

For this example, we are going to make our own username be PERSON1. You can then decide what information can be inside of the PERSON1 database, and you can even start up your own table that is just going to work with this username, maybe we will call it EMPLOYEES_TBL to make it easier. To see a bit more about how this works, when you decide to go into the records, you will notice that with this table, it is going to be labeled as PERSON1 EMPLOYEES_TBL. This is how others are going to see the name of the table as well because it helps them to know who is responsible for creating the table. The schema here is going to be the same, but it will include the username that was chosen, and then the name of the table that they pick as well.

When anyone is trying to access the schema that belongs to them, you will not need to list out the exact name of the schema that they are in. you would just need to pull up the name that was given to the table. So, for the example that we took some time on before, you would just need to pull up EMPLOYEES_TBL. The schema already knows what your username is, and it knows that you do not have access to the other tables, so the PERSON1 is not necessary with this.

Creating a new table

When it comes to working with databases, it is important to create lots of tables, ones that make sense and can store information for you in a neat and orderly fashion. There are a lot of different tables that you are able to use with the SQL language, so having a good understanding of them will make it easier. And the first thing that we are going to do in order to work with these tables and make sure that they can hold onto the information that you want is to create our first table.

Any time that you would like to create your own table in the SQL language, you will just need to use the command CREATE TABLE. It is as simple as that (remember we said SQL was easy to learn and write out!). This is the command that you can use to bring up the table and start using it, but we do need to take a few more steps before you are able to fill it in with the information that you need. This simply makes sure that we get the framework of the table set up so that it is ready for the writing later.

Before you use this command though, you have to stop and think about the way that you would like to have the table look, the kind of information that you plan to add to the table, how bit the table needs to be, along with any other information that may influence the final product of your table. Don't worry though, no matter which version of the SQL language you decide to work with, there will be options here that help you to create the table you want, even if you have no experience with this at all.

Creating a table based on one that already exists

The next thing that we need to look at is how you would be able to create a brand new table that is based on the information that you would be able to find in another table that was already written. There will be some times with this language where you have some information from an older table that you would like to keep and use for information to make a new one. This can save you a lot of time when you need to reorganize the information that you have and when you want to make sure the table comes out looking nice in the end.

The commands that you will need to do with this one will start out with CREATE TABLE as we used before, and then you will also need the command of SELECT. Once you have been able to work with both of these commands, you will see that it is responsible for creating a new table, one that has the same definitions and parameters as the old table you are copying from.

This can be a great feature that makes your database creation easier and will save you some time as well as potential mistakes. This is a good one that can help you to create a brand new table that you can then change up and customize the way that you want, while still using the information that you need from the older table.

Since we are looking at a coding language here, there is going to be a little bit of coding that we have to focus on to make sure that this new table is created, and that it is going to contain the information that you need from the original table. If you want to use the old table as the basis for a new table, then the syntax that you need to use to make this happen includes:

CREATE TABLE NEW_TABLE_NAME AS
SELECT [*/COLUMN1, COLUMN2]
FROM TABLE NAME
[WHERE];

As you look back at the syntax that we have above, you should be able to see that the two parts that we talked about above, the fact that you need the CREATE TABLE and the SELECT commands, were used in this, so we know that we did most of it right (or at least this part). The SELECT keyword is perfect to use here because it is the command that you are able to use any time that you are working on a query for a particular database. This keyword is going to work to make sure that the new table will be created the way that you want, using the search results to get this done.

How to drop the tables you don't want

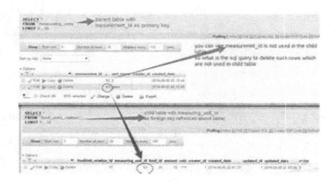

One final topic that we need to take a look at here when we work on the SQL language is how we are able to go through and drop tables. If you are able to use a brand new keyword that we are going to introduce now the RESTRICT keyword, and then you reference the table that you want by using the constraint or the view that you set up, you will be well on your way. Often you are going to see the keyword DROP used with this one too, but this can often give you more of an error signal in your system.

Another option that you can try to use with this kind of code, in addition to using the two above, would be the CASCADE command that shows up along with your DROP command. This has to happen to make sure that the DROP command is going to work in the right way and that all of the constraints and the views that are already found inside of the table you are working on will actually be dropped. An example of a code that you are able to use to make all of this happen will be below:

DROP TABLE TABLE_NAME [RESTRICT | CASCADE]

Any time that you would like to go through your database and drop a new table inside of it, you need to make sure that the program has a good idea who the owner of that table is. Sometimes the program will take the information without this part, but it is a good habit to get into because it helps to keep the database organized and will make sure that everyone has an idea of who is in charge of that new table.

Adding the name of the person who owns the table is going to help with a lot of issues including making sure that you don't lose the information or that you don't accidentally drop the wrong table in the process. If you have access to not only your own table but to other accounts as well, naming the tables properly will make sure that you don't get confused and that you are able to find the information that you need easily.

Since you will end up working with a ton of information when you do a database with SQL, it makes sense that these tables are an important part of making this kind of system work the way that you would like. The tables are going to help you not only to gather up the information that is important at that time, but they are going to present it and lay everything out in a way that is easiest to read.

From there, the tables that you create will be able to take the information, or perhaps the products that you would like to sell, and they can present them to you in a way that is easier for you and for other users to look through. Or you are able to set up the table so that the user when they are visiting the website and their own accounts, will be able to see the information laid out well.

Creating the tables in the SQL language is not supposed to be something that is difficult. We did several codes in this chapter that show us exactly how we would be able to set these up, without having to worry about it being too difficult or even worrying about how difficult it is to read the code. Creating these tables is one of the best ways to organize the information that you want to keep in your database and can make it easier to draw it out and use it at any time that you would like.

Chapter 5: Doing Your Own Search Results

We have mentioned a few times through this guidebook how people are able to get on the database for SQL and then do some search queries, you are able to do this a lot with this kind of language because it ensures that you are able to find the information that you want out of the database, without having to read every single item. You don't really want to go through and try to read through all of the items that Amazon has for sale. This is millions of products, and it could take forever before you find the product that you want. Doing a search query with the help of the SQL language will help you to get through this and find the results that actually match up what you need.

The SQL language is set up to work with searches and can be a great way for you and other users of the database to search for items and terms and make sure that the things that actually match up with that are going to show up on the screen. This is one of the fastest and most effective ways that you are able to sort through the information that you find in the database so that you make sure it is organized in the right way and to ensure that the right items that match your results show up on the screen as well here.

Once you have been able to go through the process of creating your own database or website for your business, and you have gone through the last chapter to make sure you know how to create and design the tables that you need, it is time to look through how to make your own queries and get accurate results with this system.

You have the benefit here because you are able to make the SQL language work for you to ensure that you are able to find any result that you want, as long as that information is found inside your database. Before you go through and do this though, you have to make sure that any database you plan to use is set up in the right manner so that any time you do one of these queries, the right information is going to show up without any problems.

One of the best ways for you to think about this process is that at times, someone is going to come and check out your website because they want to find a particular type of product that you have available. In this case, are you more interested in providing them with a database that is slow or will give those results that are not accurate? This may turn out to be the least expensive method in many cases, but it is just going to result in the user getting angry and frustrated. And with all of the competition that is out there, it is also likely that the user is going just to find another company to purchase from, and you will lose out on a sale.

A better option is to make sure that the database is set up in the proper manner so that it works quickly, and it will provide the user with the results that they are looking at. And that is what we are going to focus on inside of this chapter. Our job here is to learn some of the best codes and practices that you can use in order to set up the queries that you are using and get them to work well in the database while providing the best results for you.

How to create your own query

So, the first place to start here is to look at the best way to create a query in the SQL language. Before you start writing out your queries, just remember that when you send out this query, you are sending out information so that it reaches to a database that you set up previously. You want to make sure that the right command, which is the SELECT command, is the part used in this query, no matter what you plan to lookup.

Let's take a look at an example of how this is going to work. You may be working with one table, and the responsibility of that table is to hold onto the products that you listed out in the database. To help you get this done, you would need to use the SELECT command, and then the products are all going to be listed out for you. Of course, it is likely that the user is going to want a specific product that you are selling, so then they would need to type in the product they want, along with some of the other specifications they want, such as a price point and more, and then submit. If the database is set up in the proper manner, they will end up getting the results that they want.

Understanding the SELECT command a bit more

We have already spent a bit of time talking about the importance of the SELECT command and how this is going to make sure that we are able to read through the database that we have. Anytime that you are trying to work with the website, or you need to go into the database and create a new query, you will need to bring out that SELECT command to make it all happen. This command is really versatile, and it is going to take over the task of starting and executing any queries that you plan to send out to the databases.

To make this easy, you need to work with the SELECT command and then add in something to the statement to tell the database exactly what you are looking for. Sending out just the SELECT command will not tell the database what you want. You are able to add in any kind of search time that you would like after the command, but make sure it is there to help the command know where to search in the database.

Any time that you want to bring out this kind of command in the SQL language, there are going to be four main keywords that are important and will be a part of this process as well. We are going to take a look at these. Keep in mind that these four keywords are going to be referred back to as the four clauses so if you hear them by that name, we are talking about the same thing. The four clauses that you may encounter as you work with this command include:

SELECT

This is the command that you can use as long as it is combined with the command FROM. When these two keywords are put together, they are going to make sure that you have the right data, and that this data is put into a format that is organized and easy to read. You will need to use these two keywords in order to determine what kind of data is going to show up.

The clause SELECT is going to introduce the different columns that you need to see with the search results, and then you need to work with the clause of FROM to find the exact points in the table that you need at this point.

FROM

We just mentioned the FROM clause a bit before, but it is important to spread it out into its own place. Remember from before that the SELECT and the FROM clause all need to work together to get the query done the way that you would like. The reason that both of these must show up together is that it takes the search from doing the whole database, down to just the actual things that you want to find in the database.

If you went through and did the query without the help of both of these clauses together, it is likely that you would have to search through all of the results that were in the database. If the business only had twenty items for sale altogether, then this may not be that big of a deal. But if they have a million items for sale, it is not likely that the customer, or even you, will want to sort through all of the results until you were able to find the one that you wanted.

When the SELECT and the FROM clause works together, you will find that this is no longer a problem. It will limit down the information that you need in the database, making it so that only the results that match up with the query are going to show up on the screen.

For this process to work, you need to have a minimum of one FROM clause. To help us learn a bit how this is going to work and how everything is going to come together with these two keywords, let's take a look at the syntax of an SQL code that will use both the FROM and SELECT keywords in the proper manner.

SELECT [*\ ALL| DISTINCT COLUMN1, COLUMN2]
FROM TABLE1 [, TABLE2]:

WHERE

The next keyword that we need to take a look at is the one WHERE. This is the one that you will need to use when you see more than one condition inside of the clause. A good example of this one is the element that shows up in the query that will display any of the data that is selective after the user has been able to put in any information they wish to find.

If you have decided to work with this kind of feature, there are going to be two other conditions that are proper to use here, and they include the OR and the AND operators. The best syntax to use to work with the WHERE command will include the following:

SELECT [* \ALL\ DISTINCT COLUMN1, COLUMN2]
FROM TABLE1 [, TABLE2]:
WHERE [CONDITION1 \ EXPRESSION 1]
[AND CONDITION2 \ EXPRESSION2]

ORDER BY

And the fourth clause that we are going to take a look at is the ORDER BY clause. You will be able to work this particular clause if it is time to arrange some of the output of the query that you did. The server is able to decide the format and the order of the information that the user will see when they are done with a basic query. If the user does not go through and determine the order type that they want, then the default for this will be to provide the output from A to Z.

This doesn't mean that you are stuck with this. You can go through and write out the information so that it shows up in any order that you would like, just make sure that it is done ahead of time if you want something other than the default. The syntax that you can use with this one will use the code that we wrote in the las last section, but then you need to add the line below to the end of it to make this work:

ORDER BY COLUMN1 | INTEGER [ASC/DESC]

All of these will need to be in place with your code if you would like to make sure that the command of SELECT is going to work in the proper manner and to ensure that it will be able to go through the database and pull out information that actually matches, or is similar, to the query you did about that database.

Working with the case sensitivity

The next topic that we need to take a look at is how case sensitivity is going to work with this language, and whether or not it is something that you need to worry about. The nice thing about working in the SQL language is that the case sensitivity is not going to matter as much, at least not as much as it does with some other coding languages that you can work with. You can choose to work with lower case and upper case letters, any of them that you would like because they will be viewed the same in any query that you do. You even get the choice of looking at the statements and the clauses and see the different ways that they will show up in the code.

Now, with this information said, there may be a few times in this language was the case sensitivity is going to be important. For example, you may have a time when you are in a situation where there are some data objects. You find that mostly, the data that you plan to use is all written out using upper case letters.

The reason that this happens is that it is done to let other users see something is consistent in the code, and they will know why. If you add in any other objects to that database, it is often best if you are able to list them out in upper case letters. Not because this is going to make that much of a difference, but it ensures that the information all look uniform and consistent.

Without this rule in place, may find that someone would get onto the database and use the term JOHN one time, but then another user would come on and use John, and then a third would go with john and so on. A beginner who is working on this language may run into trouble understanding whether these are the same thing or not, or if the users are talking about the same person here and this gets a bit confusing.

In the long run, it is better to have it all in uppercase letters in the code so that it matches, and it can make sure that everyone is always on the same page when it comes to using this kind of code. It also helps to prevent some potential issues that could come up otherwise.

The reason that those who developed SQL decided to work with the uppercase format, rather than something else, is because the uppercase letters are easier to read, and it is going to match up with what you may have done in some of the other databases that you may have done in the past. If you choose that the uppercase method is not really the best one for you, then at least make sure that your labeling and naming system is as consistent as possible to avoid some issues.

Another thing that we need to consider when we are working with some transactions in our database is that you will do a lot of queries and transactions with all of this as well. We talked about some of these before, but it is possible that the queries and the transactions are going to go together in some cases. These transactions are going to be important, although you may feel that this includes information that the user is not that interested in.

However, if you find that the case sensitivity is not used properly, or you don't take the time to check that the table is set up in the manner that you should have it, then you will end up with the results being wrong after the query. And this leads to unhappy customers who will not want to come back and check out your website ever again.

Any time that you decide to create a new database, and you want to work inside of it, you need to make sure that you have set up the query as well as possible ahead of time. This takes a few extra minutes when you are doing this, but it makes it so much easier for the user to find whatever they are looking for inside of your database. No one wants to come to your website and then find that it is too hard to get the information that they need. And working with the case sensitivity in the proper manner can sometimes be the reason that the code is not working the way that you would like.

Let's pretend that you are going to one of your favorite sights to look up some items that you would like to get. You have an idea of what you want, and you type it into the search query. How do you feel when you are able to find the right item that you want, with all of the right specifications, within the first few results that come up on the page? It is likely that you feel good and are appreciative that it doesn't take as much of your time to do this. You may even be more likely to come back to the website again and make another purchase.

On the other hand, how are you going to feel if you do the same thing, but the results come back nothing as you want? You try out four or five different keywords along the way, and nothing is matching up the way that you want. You look through pages of information, and it still doesn't give you the results that you want. When this happens, it is easy to get frustrated and mad, and you may get upset with the company and not want to work with them again.

This is the same idea when we are working with case sensitivity and getting this language to work with what you want. You are in business to make the customers happy, and if they are unhappy because your database is not working in the manner that you would like, then this is going to be a big problem that you need to fix.

This is why working with the queries that you need and making sure that they end up working in the proper manner and communicating with the database in the right manner is critical to ensuring the website works and that your customers are happy. Your ultimate goal here is that when the user visits your website and types in some kind of keyword for a search, that they are only getting items that closely match, and nothing else. This helps to make sure that the customer is going to be happy, and can help to build up your reputation as a business.

There are many people who will work with this kind of database to help them list out the products that they want customers to purchase. Even if this is the way that you plan on working on this database, there may still be some times when the search function could be useful, and you still want to make sure that it is functioning properly.

For example, if the user wants to come to your website, and they wish to look through the database and find specific information, such as their account information or the payment method that they like to use, or even the services you provide, it is still important that you have the query search set up in such a manner that this search is easy and that the user will find the information, even if they may not use the query as much as some other options.

As someone who is just getting started with the SQL language, it is important to realize how important some of these queries are and why you want to make sure that the SQL query is going to show up where it belongs, rather than giving a lot of information that the user does not need. No matter how you are using the database, these queries are going to be an integral part of the work that you are doing.

Chapter 6: Relational Database Concepts

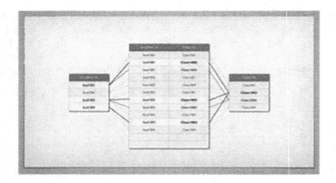

The next thing that we are going to explore when it comes to working with the SQL language is the idea of the relational database. The database engine that powers SQL is going to be strong, and it does have the ability to make decisions on its own, without the programmer there, thanks to the user-input instructions. The language of SQL, which is called Transact-SQL (also known as T-SQL) will contain some of the basic objects that are needed to define these data requests.

Literal values are going to be constant in your code, no matter what you are doing, and you may find that they will include numeric, hex, or alphanumeric values that will be turned into a string and enclosed into some single quotes. It is possible that you will need to work with double quotes here, but there are other uses for these quotes other than using this, and most coders are going to just stick with the single quotations to make things easier.

We also need to look at the delimited identifiers. These are there because inside of the code they will reserve specific keywords, while also enabling the objects of the database to contain names that include a space in them. The default that we see with these kinds of statements are going to use the double quotes that we talked about before. However, manipulation of this kind of setting can happen if you use the SET statement.

In some instances, there may be a statement that the engine of the database will not need to process at all, and it is important to look at these as well. Notating the lines that the code doesn't need to process will include having an asterisk and the forward-slash on both sides of the lines. So an example of this would be something like /* this is a quote */ will render the text between the notation as a comment.

There are a lot of codes out there that are going to use the idea of the comments to help get things done. These are basically like little notes that show up in your code, that let you and other coders know what is happening in the code, but will not affect the work that is taking place. If you want to name a particular part of the code, or you want to leave a note for another coder about the code, then you would use the comments that you would like without having to worry about it ruining the code or hurting any of the queries that are set with the program either.

In this language, the identifiers are going to be used to reference some of the diverse resources that are present including the database, the objects, and the tables, providing users with a new shorthand method that they can use in order to request the complex data that is found in the query. Of course, there are going to be a specific syntax that you need to implement and define them properly.

The nice thing about working with these identifiers is that they will be able to add in some complexity to any query string that you do, simply because they can introduce the variable syntax rules. Identifiers can start with pretty much any kind of character that you would like. But once you have been able to set these, you need to make sure that the names are chosen carefully so that they won't be called out on accident. And like many of the other languages that are out there, there will be some reserved keywords, which have reserved meanings and can only be used to call up commands and actions inside of the language.

Creating data that you are able to reference back is going to mean that we need to adhere to certain processes and that some level of consistency needs to be present the whole time. This can happen when you limit the data that is inside of a column to just one type of data, and no more. Of course, there can always be exceptions to this based on the kind of program that you are trying to create, but for the most part, each column in the database or in a table needs to just have one single data type in it.

Numeric data is just fine in the database. Sometimes this is used to represent various forms of counted data including decimal, integer, real, and money depending on the program you are working with. All of these are numerical data and basically means that you will fill in that particular column of the database with some kind of number in the process.

You can then go with some character data containers. These are going to be available in both a variable and a fixed-length strip. If you want just to let the person put in the abbreviation for the state, then you would limit these containers to two parts. If you want to let them pick out a unique password, or you want them to write out their whole name without any restrictions, then you would use the variable character.

Then there are some of the Unicode store containers. These are going to take the character strings that have a byte that is bigger than one. Data related to time is going to be called temporal data, and it is important because it is able to concern date and time information that is stored in different sizes and with different specifics attached to each one. You will find that most of the data types that are temporal are not going to understand things like time zones or daylight savings time, but the DATETIMEOFFSET is able to define a type of data that is able to accommodate the time zones if it is needed to manipulate the data at hand.

You may find that this language will allow you to also work with different types of data that may not fit into the three categories that we were talking about at all. But they do still need to fit into some of the other parameters, including things like SQL-variant, large objects, and binary data to name a few.

Another thing that we need to take a look at here is how the SQL language is going to enlist two kinds of functions, which are known as the scalar and the aggregate. First, we will take a look at the aggregate function. As we can guess by the name, this data is going to be contained within one single column, and because of this, it is going to return just one value for the query. It is possible to work with several types of these functions, including user-defined, analytical, statistical, and convenient.

An example of working with the aggregate function is going to be when we use the SUM function. This SUM function is going to calculate out the total value of all the entries that you are able to find in a single column. This function, in particular, is going to be known as a convenient function, and the complexity of what you are able to do with this is going to be staggering when you form queries that can apply some of the other functions, especially when we take a look at what this is able to do with some of the user-defined aggregate functions.

Then we need to take a look at the scalar functions. These are going to be divided up into five categories, and they will operate on a single row or a singular value as opposed to an aggregate function which will run on many rows inside just one column. There are actually hundreds of these functions that can come into use when we talk about data manipulation, but to keep it simple we will break them down into metadata, system, string, date, and numeric functions.

Functions are going to manipulate the data, and then the numeric functions are able to transform the data using some of the instructions that are mathematical. The date functions are able to perform some calculations on the date and the time of your formulated data. And then we have the string function which is going to include things like shaping character string data.

We can then take a look at the system functions that are a bit more varied than what we find with other options, and these are going to provide us with some information about the objects that are found in the database. These functions are not going to be able to take the data and transform it as much as some of the other options, but they are important because they will give us the information that we need to figure out the state of our database and how this database is doing.

And finally, we need to take a look at the metadata functions. This is also going to follow this form while providing us information regarding the state of our database. These functions are going to help us by retrieving all of the names and the IDs of objects in the database. You will see that things like data types, tables, views, schemas, databases, and database files are going to be the primary concern when it comes to the metadata functions. In some cases, you are able to use this kind of function to allow for the retrieval of values for a given property without the objects of the database, within the database itself, or even in the instance of the server.

Operators that are inside this language are going to be scalar, and they will be able to apply to the mathematical and the Boolean operations, including the concatenation. Concatenation is going to be a database context that is meant to refer back to the joining together of many tables, fields, or objects. Operator types that fall into this can include binary and unary arithmetic, bitwise, set operators, logic operators, compound, comparison, and more.

Of course, we need to have a look at some of the operators that are used here to make sure that we can manipulate the data as we want. Some of the symbols that help us to do this manipulation will include OR, NOT, and AND. These can work on any function across all of the types of data that you want to work with.

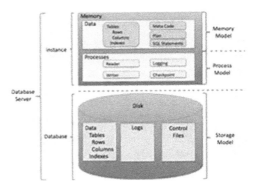

We are not going to be able to list out all of the operators that are available with this because there are too many to include without getting too technical with this work and most of the models and their usage are going to be beyond the scope of what we are trying to do with this book. The most important thing to note with this is that there are a lot of possibilities that you can consider and as familiarity with this language increases, encountering some of the operators that are seen as the most common will happen all of the time.

If you need to learn a bit more about how these operators work and how you can make sure that you get the most out of it, you will find that both ORACLE and Microsoft are going to present us with some free education about these operators and how to use them the way that you need.

The next things that we need to take a look at are the NULL values and the global variables. These are going to require some inclusion into some of the more essential components of SQL. First, we will look at the global variables. These are going to be used in place of the constants in the code, and you will need to proceed them by @@ to show that a global variable is inserted there.

NULL values are also going to be a significant feature of working in SQL. Even though relational meddles are going to require that all data is referenceable in the real world practice, there are times when some unknown data is going to show up, and the NULL value allows you to create a table still, and manipulate it the way that you would like, without all of the information in the table is present each time.

Understanding the basics of this languages data type functions and the objects will provide a base of knowledge that will expand into the progressively more specific areas of database creation and manipulation. Going through this chapter and looking through what each of these parts is in this chapter to help you get the results that you want with this coding.

Chapter 7: How to Define Data in SQL

The next thing that we need to focus on when it comes to SQL is how to define some of the data that we are using in SQL. Defining the databases means that we need to be able to use the right statements in this language that relates back to the data definition language. Operations that are related to deletion, modification, and creation are the three segments of this kind of language that we need to look through.

To start, the organization of our database is going to comprise of many different types of objects. You can have either logical or physical objects based on the data that you are working with and the device that the user is working with as well. And even though it can seem a bit redundant, the database is going to be part of the organization of the database. What this means is that the database itself is one of the objects that we can work with, and when the right statement is used, you will be able to manipulate this object as well.

Of course, it is impossible to go through and work with a database if you don't first have a database object in place first. And the two main methods that you can use to make this happen include CREATE DATABASE, or you can even work with the SQL management studio if you are working with this language on a Microsoft product. The Oracle version is going to function in a slightly different manner, but it is still pretty straightforward to work with as well.

As you are creating a new database, remember that you need to name the database. This is going to make sure that the engine is going to be able to use this identifier to call up the database any time there is a query going on for that information. The name needs to follow the same kinds of restrictions that all of the other identifiers are going to share as we talked about before.

As you create a database, you will find that it will define the creator as the owner of the database, and then it goes through and also makes a log file that is able to track each change that is made to the database, from the moment it is created onward. Even if logging is not correctly defined yet, the system is able to generate a log file to help maintain the changes that you end up doing, mainly for the benefit of the engine of the database's logic.

Earlier in this guidebook, we talked about the data independence specified that the functionality of a database is not dependent on the logical or the physical structure. This is why it is so important to impart that the function is not going to be affected by how data is stored and accessed on the physical disk. Physical data organization does end up affecting the performance in some situations, such as when the database is really extensive.

When the database is extensive, the established methodologies are going to exist in order to create some filegroups of related databases for distribution among various physical disks to enhance how well it is able to perform.

The creation of a new database is going to allow for a template called a model. The usage of models is going to occur when a specific element or object in the database has to be present in all of the databases that you create. This is going to be set by the administrator and isn't always a necessity. The SQL database is also going to allow for a snapshot view of the database at a given interval in time if this is needed. The reason that some companies like to work with snapshots is that it is really useful to help you protect your database against any of the errors that your users may have, as well as to help you understand some of the evolution that happens in the code.

Any of the elements that are considered primary elements will be found inside the tables of the database. Your tables are going to require that you use consistent integrity in the data to make sure that it stays stable. The administrators are going to be the part of the database that comes in and maintain the consistency, but you will find that the engine for the database will provide the administrator with some tools to create any limitations to prevent some of the inconsistent entries users may do.

This is why you need to work with the database engine in a consistent manner. This feature is vital because even the administrators are going to be susceptible to some human error, but the database engine is going to be immune to some of the limitations of human error. It is possible to turn on some of these restrictions and then turn it over to the management system, either on a table wide or a per column basis based on what seems to work the best for the database you are creating.

Examples of table or column restrictions could include requiring unique clauses to identify candidate keys, and one of those potential columns is eligible to become the primary key. The primary key is going to be a column where each row of the column will contain a different value from the others. This is going to be considered the most important column in the whole table, and this will need to be set up as the basis of querying specific information based on the unique identifiers for a given database.

Foreign keys can show up as well, and these are going to be the matching identifier to a primary key, but it is going to be in a related, but a separate database. These two fields must maintain data consistency in order also to maintain their integrity. The check clause is going to help the data entry users to retain reference agreement by enforcing requirements upon insertion of new data.

The transact language in SQL is going to support you modify the structure of database objects, and some of the ones that you can modify will include the database, the table, the procedure, view, trigger, and schema. Adding or removing any of the logs in the filegroups or the files of the database is something that you will do the most option, but there are other things that you are able to do with this. SQL is going to store each of the databases on a single disk file, and the filegroup is just going to be a larger collection of these files.

Modifying the database using this method is helpful in some cases because it is going to enhance how well it performs, and can even change up some of the physical storage structure that comes with the data, without having to change up the execution of the queries. You can also choose to edit a database with the code ALTER DATABASE clause, and this statement is also responsible for setting the database options or changing the properties of the filegroup.

The database options available are going to be varied, and they will include things like a change of the state of the database including who can access it, the people who can read or write on the database, the status of access such as whether you can get it offline or only online and more. The SQL language is going to allow you to have a moving database with the help of the command for attaching and detach, but while you are able to do this, there are a lot of issues that can come up with the process.

The good news is that while that process can run you into some issues if you are not careful, Microsoft has come up with a contained database to help deal with the loss of metadata that sometimes happens with detachment. Detaching the database is going to help retain the information that you need, but then the security and the properties of the database are going to be considered separate from the data. What this resulted in was that in the past, when you moved a database, it would require a tedious amount of rebuilding the security and some of the metadata that went missing.

Thanks to the contained database that is available with Microsoft now, you are able to move the database and all of the attributes that come with it, quickly and effectively. The SQL Server 2012 is only going to support a partially contained database, but the newer versions from 2014 and on are able to have the contained database, and this is going to be a process that is similar to creating the objects of your objects.

The neat thing that comes up here is that the commands are going to be simple. All of the commands that you used for the CREATE statement will exist in duplicate when you decide to use the DROP statement in the code. But one critical aspect of dropping the objects of the database to remember is that it includes losing the data, the triggers, and the indices that are related to any of the discarded data.

Retention of the views of that database will remain dependent on the presence of the data. The "View" will then be incomplete at this point because the reference data no longer needs to exist, but you will find that the "View" is still selectable in this situation.

From here, we need to take a look at a few of the data definition statements, and in particular we need to look at the ones like ALLOW, DROP, and CREATE and how these are going to be responsible for the creation of new procedures, indices, triggers schema, views, tables, and even with new databases.

First, we have the ALTER statement for objects. This one is going to be robust when we take a look at all that it is able to accomplish, and it is going to be helpful when you would like to define the functionality of a database. There are a lot of different things that you are able to do with this statement that we won't have time for in this guidebook, but it is still important to know that the ALTER statement is going to be a good one for you to learn how to use when it comes to the functionality of the tables you are working on.

Chapter 8: Working with Indexing, Views, and Queries

Now that we have had a chance to take a look at some of the different things that you are able to work on in the SQL language, and some of the background noise that helps to make sure the database is able to work, it is time for us to explore a bit more about some of the actual actions that you are able to work with when you want to make this coding language work for you.

It is all well and good to create some of the databases and put in the information that you need along the way. You won't be able to do anything with the database if there is not a strong table and good information put into it as well. But you may find that this process is not going to do all of the things that you want until you learn how to work with a few other actions.

In this guidebook, we are going to take a look at doing queries, views, and indexing with the codes that you want to write in SQL. These are all going to be a bit different from each other, but it is something that you and the user will need to use on a regular basis to actually use and access the database that has been created. So, let's get started.

The first option that we need to take a look at queries here. These queries are simple to work with because they will work with one single statement in order to get the retrieval of the data that is needed, and that statement is SELECT. This statement is one that we have talked about a bit before in this guidebook, but it is a good idea to have some review of how it works and why it is such an important part of any code that you decide to write. Remember that the select statement includes a few different parts of the code that you need including operators, functions, and clauses.

Now, there are a lot of options when it comes to expanding out one of the queries that you are writing, and in some queries, this can make the search a bit more complex. What we mean by complex queries here is that they are going to have a lot of different parts to them. Instead of working with just "girl's dresses" for your query, for example, you may decide to add in the color, the length, how long it takes to ship, and the size and turn it into a more complex query.

SELECT statements are going to request for information from one or more table that is inside the database, or that are inside more than one database at the time. The results of a query return in a table format, which makes sure that you or the user will receive a new database table called the result set. Some of the clauses that you will be able to use when you decide to do a query will include ORDER BY, HAVING, GROUP BY, WHERE, FROM, and INTO.

We will start by looking at the WHERE clause. This one is important because it is going to define any of the conditions that will limit the rows of data that you can select. It operates more as a Boolean function where the resultant set is returned based on whether the statement is true or false, and will check the rows that you specified to find it in the first place. This clause uses Boolean results because this is going to allow for a bit more complexity by being able to add in another operator to the mix, including AND, NOT, and OR following some of the standard logic that is Boolean.

The operators also have some weights that are prioritized in the order of NOT, AND, then OR, and this is going to be important when you want to apply some logic to one of the queries that you are working on. We can then move on to some operators that are not considered Boolean, and these are going to be BETWEEN and IN, can work in conjunction with the Boolean operators to help you to delineate some of the requests that you have for the data.

When you are doing some of the work to design these queries, it is useful to help you write the query in plain language as much as possible, and then you can translate that everyday speech into logic. Another of the non-Boolean operators that you may work with, LIKE, is going to be able to tell the engine of the database to seek patterns within a column and return results based on some of the other operators that work in conjunction with it.

Then there is the clause of GROUP BY which allows for some column data to be grouped in a manner so that the query can return similar rows of data where the grouped columns end up holding onto the same type of data. Then the HAVING clause is going to be applied when groups of rows require a condition to recover data within the syntax of a query to help you out. This is often either going to be an aggregate function or a constant value, such as the sum of the columns altogether. All of the clauses of this are going to be built upon one another to increase the complexity. The logic of the HAVING clause here is going to be that it specifies a value in order to delineate information by when the GROUP BY clause returns a larger resultant set than desired.

The HAVING clause is going to limit the specific data that is going to come up when you use GROUP BY into a particular limit on that data or for that comparison of data.

We can then move over to the ORDER BY clause which is going to specify the way that the data needs to be returned when the query is done and allows for the information to show up for the user in a manner that makes the most sense. It could do something like the lowest price to highest, or even from ascending or descending order based on what you would like. It is possible for you to go through and modify the priority of the columns that are displayed, which would then allow you to change the order from the SELECT statement, or even sort the data by multiple columns at the same time.

While it may seem like these statements are confusing and that they will be too confusing when you try to work on them at the same time. But some examples that we will look at in a bit will help to clarify the situation and will make sure that we can fully use them all in the proper manner and still get the most that we can from them.

These queries are going to be important to work with because they are important for sorting through a lot of tables and databases, while getting through a ton of data that is found in them, in a quick and efficient manner. How fast they are able to do this will depend on the size and the arrangement of the database of course. If you have millions of results, it could take a bit longer for the program to actually go through the database and find the information that you want. Of course, you do have some methods available to make sure that the time it takes the system to respond is kept to a minimum. The best way to do this is to index the data so that it can be accessed faster.

The database engine is going to try to work with an optimizer for the query in order to make sure that any results it is providing are achieved more quickly with the existing indices in use, as well as deciding if some of the indexed data has been moved or modified in any other way since the last time that the language used any statements to drop, alter, or create the indexes.

If this process is done and a table is not attached, then the system is going to go through each part of the database, line for line and column for the column, in order to find the results that go with the query. As you can imagine, this is not going to really help you much because the process is tedious and can take too long. But while it is not efficient, the data is going to be processed quickly so that when the database is relatively small, the slowdown is something that you can manage.

Basically, you want to find the best way to index your database to ensure that when a query is done, it is going to be done in a manner that makes sense for the user, and the slowdown speed of that method is not really going to be that noticeable to move people.

Rows that are indexed within the index page are going to contain what is known as a pointer and an index key that will allow the database engine to scan the page more quickly, rather than trying to scan the whole table and determine the kind of data that is the most relevant. This can make it more efficient and works the best when you have large pieces of data that you need to sort through. The data structure that is found within one of these indexes is going to follow the B-tree organization.

What is a B-tree? These are going to be a self-balancing data structure that is able to sort through the data and allows for queries, insertions, deletions, and insertions of information in the form of keys, along with some other parent and child leaves as needed. The indices will take two different forms when you are working with them in SQL, and the two forms are going to include non-clustered and clustered.

First, we need to take a look at the clustered indexes. These are the ones that are going to determine the physical order of the data that is found in the table. Only one of these types can exist per table because it is physically impossible to order data in more than one way.

From there, the leaf nodes are going to contain the data pages, while the rest of the tree that you are able to find will comprise of the index pages pointing to where the relevant data locations are within the nested structure. Now, there are also indexes that are known as non-clustered, and these come in pretty much the same kind of structure that we talked about before, but there are two main differences that we have to know that sets these apart.

First, when you are working with a non-clustered index, you will notice that it is not going to be able to actually change the physical location where you find data in the table, and then the leaf page that comes with this is not going to contain any of the actual data that you are going to use. Instead of all this, the leaves are basically like bookmarks in the code and the index keys. These bookmarks are important to the code because they will make the database more efficient and will provide a direct shortcut to your queried data.

It is possible to have some of these non-clustered parts work at the same time as the clustered indexes, but it is also possible that they may work on their own when you bring them into a database. It all depends on the kind of program that you are trying to create for your needs.

At times, you will find that these indexes are going to become more fragmented with use from you. The more times that the data is retrieved and then stored again, it is possible that this is done in a manner that is not that efficient, and things start to break up and become fragmented. Taking some time on occasion to reorganize the information is a good option any time that you fear the fragmentation of the data is more severe. Indexing is a vital part of your database and can make sure that the code is going to work the way that you would like to see it work.

Another core competency that we need to take a moment to study here is all about creating and then leveraging the views that you have. To keep this as simple as possible, the view is going to be another name that we are going to give for a virtual table. A base table is always going to exist inside of your physical store, but then you can also have a virtual table, as long as you make sure that you do not index it and you make sure that it doesn't take up any storage in your data.

Views are going to be a kind of object that is found in the database, and you will see that it is derived from some of the base tables thanks to the help of the metadata that we talked about before. The creation of a new view can source from a separate virtual table, but there are a few reasons that make it beneficial to create one of your one.

You will find that sometimes, a query is going to be a bit more complicated, and you can simplify these with the help of a virtual table that is able to correspond back to the query for the database, the one that you or another user typed in, to begin with. The relationship that is going to show up here can reveal an important fact that we need to look at with views and this is that the views are going to come from a resultant set of data that is then returned by the query that was used.

A good way to help with this issue is to try and limit the scope of the values that your users are able to modify and update can be another reason here. If you make it so that each user is only able to create or change certain parts of the database, rather than the whole thing, you prevent someone from just coming in and messing up the database, and you also make sure that human error when it comes to importing data into your database, will be kept away, or at least down to a minimum.

Queries are going to be an important part of any coding that you do in the SQL database. You will find that a lot of people are going to want to master this skill because it allows them to make sure that everything comes up in the right manner. There is no way that you or one of your users will want to actually go through and manually read through all of the results that come with your database, but when the query is set up the right way, then this ensures that the right results come up each time.

With this in mind, we talk about indexes. These are basically going to help leave a little bookmark behind so that the query is able to find the information that it needs as well. They may not be necessary, but when you are working with an SQL database that is relatively big in size, it can make the search more efficient and more accurate overall, so it is definitely worth your time to learn how to use these as well.

This chapter has contained a lot of the information that we need to know in order to create some of the best codes for our needs. But there is definitely a lot of new information to go through and taking the time to check out all of the things that you are able to do with the SQL language, and how you can work with some of the databases that are found with this one can make a world of difference as well.

As we talked about in this guidebook a little bit, creating queries, leveraging, indexing, and establishing some pertinent views that make sense from a business intelligence perspective are really a big core component that comes with those who want to work with SQL. There is so much that you are able to do with the help of this kind of database, and it helps to keep all of your information so organized, that it makes sense to have it as part of your own business organization as well.

Of course, since we have gone through a lot of different topics during this chapter, it is also natural to feel a bit overwhelmed and like this is a lot of information to take in! The best way to master these skills is to work on them a bit and practice. SQLite is an application that you are able to get for free that will make sure that a new user to SQL is able to get started easily and gain some of the experience that you need to really see what the database is able to do on its own.

Chapter 9: Database Security

As you work with some of the databases that your business needs, you will find that the topic of security is going to come up. You have to make sure that you are able to give your customers the security that they need. They are not going to be all that happy if you decide to work on their information and you ask them to store it with you, but then you are not able to keep the information that they provide to you safely.

Think about all of the personal information that a business could hold onto for their customers. If you have a customer who makes a purchase with you and saves their information into an account, it is likely that you have some information including their name, address, phone number, and credit card number to name a few. This may not seem like that big of a deal because this is the information that the customer had to provide to you to complete the purchase. But if this information gets into the wrong hands, it could be a big headache for the customer, and the end of your business for you.

It is your job to make sure that any time you have a database that stores your customers' information for them that you are doing whatever you can to keep the information private and secure. But how are you supposed to use SQL to make sure that this security is in place over the database?

Databases are going to be containers that are able to maintain all kinds of data, corporate secrets, employee data that is sensitive, list of employees that are scheduled out for separation, customer payment information, and other types of information that no one outside of the company should really have access too. It is common for many companies to use Microsoft's active directory to help them manage users and to sort them into access profiles using a group them into a group policy process.

The way that this works in practice, and when it is used properly, is that the employees of a company are going to be given an assigned group permission based on the job title that they have, and within those permissions, there is also the possibility for more individualized permissions depending on the rank that the employee has in the group. This ensures that the company is able to control who gets to do what based on their position and ranking within the company.

You will see that the SQL is going to interact back with the Active Directory for some of the access control, but it is not going to be able to provide any internal security when it comes to the authorization. The application that comes with SQL is going to provide these services for you. As we go through this, you will notice that with the SQL database, there are going to be four main components that come into play with database security. And these are going to include authentication, authorization, encryption, and access control. Let's take a look at each of these to see how they are able to help us out when it comes to the security of our database.

First on the list is the authentication. This is going to pertain to validating whether or not a user has the right permissions to access any of the resources that are on the system in the first place. One of the most common methods that you may see when it comes to authentication is going to be the idea of the username and password. You will then be able to verify the credentials by the username and the password to determine if the user is supposed to be on the system or not.

There is a lot of potentials that can come with this method. The company gets some freedom on the rules for the username and passwords to add in a new layer of security as well. You can also choose to go with a single sign-on system if you would like. These systems are going to use the idea of certificate authentication that the user is not actually going to interact within a direct manner. The end-user will find that their system is prepared to deal with the information that provides authentication automatically, without needing to have a prompt come up or the user to do anything.

As you can imagine, many companies are going to take great steps to make sure that their system and who is able to access it, is going to be authenticated and appropriately authorized all of the time. Then the encryption is going to help make sure that this access control is strengthened a bit more because it scrambles the data into indecipherable gibberish to any potential interceptors as the data is moved between the company and the user.

There are different types of encryption that can be used on the program, but for Microsoft, you will find that the RSA encryption type is going to be used in order to protect the data. This RSA is going to be an encryption algorithm that is going to use a layered hierarchical structure along with key management in order to secure data as needed.

It is important to have both of these parts present in the authentication process. The first one will ensure that any user who is trying to get onto the database is supposed to do so. The second one makes sure that the information that is sent over to the user is going just to reach them, and won't get intercepted along the way. This is the best way to make sure that the data stays between the company and the user who requested it.

The second part of database security that we need to take a look at includes the authorization. This is going to be a process that is used in order to determine which resources that are in the system are accessible by the user. Once the client has been able to provide the right credentials, the next step is to decide which entities the subject has permission to modify or access.

Just because a user has a password and username doesn't mean that they can access every part of the system. Usually, they are going to be restricted to the information that directly pertains back to them, but they wouldn't be allowed to access the information of someone else's account unless they were the administrator. This helps to make sure that users are only able to see the information that pertains to them, and to no one else, and can keep the information as secure as possible.

In addition, SQL is going to use change tracking to maintain a good log of all the actions that could potentially come from unauthorized users. It is possible to track the activities of the authorized users if you would like, but this isn't really a part of the security functionality that comes with change tracking. Super-users or power-users that have elevated permissions could have more access and may be able to get into all of the systems, but this doesn't necessarily authorize them as users of the database. Tracking changes helps to protect the system from any operations that may be done by users who have more elevated credentials than other users.

SQL is going to rely on a security model that is comprised of three models, and all three of these models are able to interplay with one another. The three models that you can work with include permissions, principals, and securable the first one that we need to focus on here is going to be the principals. These users are going to have permission in order to access some specific objects in the system. Then the securable will refer to any of the resources that are within the database that the system is going to regulate the access of and only certain users are able to get to it. And then there is the idea of permission that is the right of a user to delete, edit, or view some of the other parts. The permission is usually either limited, yes, or no.

This is a security model that belongs to the Microsoft SQL Server, but there are going to be similar equivalents that are found on other versions of SQL management products. The theories behind modeling access control are going to be widespread through the IT industry, and they have been designed in a way that will cover much more than just the security of the database. These are some of the same principles that you are able to find behind nearly all of the enterprise applications that are going to house some sensitive data.

The security that comes with the database you use is so important. It doesn't really matter the version of SQL that you choose to work with. They all require that you have some form of security that comes with them, and this will ensure that you get the results that you want because companies want to make sure that their information is safe and that no one who doesn't have access to the account is able to get ahold of it.

Security is an important subject when it comes to the SQL database, and many companies are trying to find new ways that they are able to maintain this kind of security when they work on the database. There are a lot of books out there to talk about how to make this security even stronger, but the goal of this chapter is to do some of the most relevant topics to help you learn why the security is so important, and how you can make sure that the security is as strong as possible.

To start here, we talked about the schema a bit in some of the previous chapters, but this is also going to be something that is important for helping to define the ownership of the resources, and it can identify the principals by deciding how the user is related back to the owner. To keep this easy, the way that Microsoft defines the schema is going to be "a collection of database objects that are owned by a single person and form a single namespace."

It is important to know about the namespace because it is going to refer to the limitation that doesn't allow two tables in the same schema to go in with the same name. Data consistency and the referential ease are going to be some of the guiding ideas that come in with the design of SQL, and this is why we need to have some of the limitations in place.

It is possible to have a principal that is a single user or a single login, but it is also possible to have them be designed as a group principle. Multiple users who are sharing one role are going to be grouped together using group policy, and all can cooperatively own a schema, or they could each of their own and add all of these schemas to the same account.

It is also possible for you to take a schema and transfer it from one principle to another. When you decide to do this, it is not going to require you to rename unless the new owners maintain a schema that would end up with a duplication in the name. There are statements in this language that are meant to manage the schema, but a majority of this is going to belong back to the database administrators, rather than the principles on that system.

Another layer of security that you are able to work with will be the roles. These are used in order to identify access dependent on the title of the user and their responsibilities. There are going to be a lot of choices when it comes to the roles that are available. SQL comes with fixed server roles and a fixed role in the database, which will provide you with some implicit permissions that you do not even need to set because they will do the work for you.

Another thing that you can do here is to go through and create some of the customized application roles that you want, user-defined server roles, and even user-defined database roles. It all depends on what kind of roles you would like to see inside of your system, and what makes the most sense for your business.

These roles are going to make sure that the right users are doing the tasks that they need to within the program. If someone has a lower role in the company, for example, some of their access to the system is going to be more restricted. They may be able to view the system, but wouldn't be able to make changes to the system, or they will only be allowed in certain parts of the system. It all depends on how you set up the roles in your database.

As you can see with this one is that the roles are going to be an important part of the security that comes with your database. All of the other functions of security that you are going to try and work with will be built upon these roles. Authentication is going to help us determine who is able to access the database. The authorization is going to determine which principles have access to each schema. Then we have the encryption which will ensure that data sent between the user and the system is not intercepted from those who are outside of the company. This can also help to make sure that no potential hazards happen internally in the system either.

Sensitive data that leaks internally or that is intercepted unintentionally is going to be more dangerous than some of the external threats that are out there. This is why the roles are so important because they will maintain the information about which users are allowed to perform any given operation within a particular database.

If you are using the version of SQL that comes with Microsoft, you will find that this version is going to teach some of the security principals that are going to provide the user with the least amount of access that is possible while still letting them do their duties. This means that you will not give the user any more access to the system than they need because this ensures that no one is gaining more access than they need and prevents some security issues. If the person doesn't need access to something to do their job, then there is no reason for them to have access to it and this teaching will say that you restrict that to keep the system as safe as possible.

This kind of theory is going to prevent users from having any access to resources that they don't need to use and that they are not really trained to use. The same guiding ideas are going to be used when you work with all of the other versions of SQL as well. The purpose of the roles as we have discussed in this chapter is to limit the amount of access an employee has to the database that does not actually pertain to the work or responsibilities that they have inside of that schema.

In this system, the owners are going to be seen as "sysadmins," but all of the users of the database are going to end up with some specialized functions based on their training and some of the experience that they have.

To make sure that the security is properly in place inside of the system, the database administrators are often going to be a part of the IT department. This allows them to routinely check on the database and make sure that everything is working the way that it should and that nothing strange is going on, every employee or user is on the system in the right manner, and that no threats are present in the system.

While the database administrators are going to be part of the company's IT department, the owners of the database are not usually found in this department. This allows for a level of autonomy, which is actually necessary because administrators are going to be responsible for maintaining the structure and the consistency of many different databases, the number of which depends on the size of the company and what they are trying to do. These roles and these rules are all there for the end goal of making sure that the database is as secure and consistent as possible.

Security is going to be so important when you are working with one of your own databases in your company. You want to make sure that only the right people are able to get the information that they need, and that no one is stealing the information or gaining access to information and to the system when they have to no reason to be there at all.

The way that you do the security is going to depend on the type of system and database that you are using, and who you would like to have on the system doing each task. The best theory to go with to ensure that only the right people are going to gain access to the different parts of the database is to make sure that they only access the amount of the system that they need in order to get their job done, and nothing more.

This can make it seem harsh, and sometimes it may be a pain always to have to change up the roles and the authorization that you will allow the employee to have when they are on the system, but it is going to make a big difference in the security that is present. You will be able to change things up as you want if roles and responsibilities end up changing, but limiting some of this is going to be the safest and most secure bet.

In addition, when you create a new database for your business, it is always a good idea to set up a username and password protocol that your employees are able to pick. Make sure though that there are some rules to add to the security. You don't want someone in the company to pick out a password that is easy to guess and can compromise the whole system. Having them stick with a minimum number of characters, asking them to have a mixture of symbols, numbers, and letters can help, and even requiring a password change a few times a year can help to keep the information as safe as possible.

While talking about the database security with your IT department, make sure that you discuss the idea of encryption with them. You do not want the information to end up going over to an authorized user, to find out that someone outside of the system was able to read all of that confidential information. The right encryption is going to ensure that the information gets jumbled up and impossible to read so that only the user who is supposed to have that information will be the one who is able to read that information.

As you can see, there are a number of different methods that you are able to use when it comes to making sure that your database is as safe and secure as possible with the SQL coding language. Doing this and getting everything organized, ensuring the right authorizations are in place, and limiting how much information an individual user is able to see will ensure that your database is going to stay as safe and secure as possible.

Chapter 10: How to Use This in Real-World Situations

Now that we have taken some time to look at the SQL database, and some of the different codes and more that you are able to do with this system, it is time to take a more practical approach to this. It is time to take a look at some of the ways that you are able to use SQL in the real world, and how this can benefit your business and more.

When we look at some of the practical situations, it is common to set that databases are going to be used by more than one user, and this is often at the same time. A database that is able to support many users at once has a high level of concurrency within it. This concurrency, in some cases, will be able to lead to a loss of data or the reading of data that is not really present.

This can be a big issue to deal with depending on the kind of database that you are using. SQL is great because it is going to manage these kinds of situations with the help of transactions to control things like the durability, isolation, consistency, and atomicity that comes in some databases over time. These elements are going to comprise all of the properties that you need to look at during the transaction.

This brings up the question of what the transaction is going to be. This transaction is going to basically be a sequence of T-SQL statements that are going to combine logically and then are able to complete an operation that, in other situations, would introduce inconsistency to the database. Atomicity is a property that acts as a container for these transaction statements as you work on this. If the statement is able to successfully complete their work, then the total transaction is going to be completed.

For the most part, SQL is successful with the work that they are going to do, but if there is some part of the transaction that, for one reason or another, is not able to process fully, then the whole of the operation is going to fail, and all of the partial changes that showed up are going to head back to their previous state so you don't end up with issues or mistakes that happen.

Transactions are going to take place once a row, or they can be in a page-wide lock is in place. Locking is important because it is going to make sure that other users are not able to come into the database and make modifications to that particular part of the database. It is basically the same as reserving some spots inside of your database to make changes.

If you have locked that part of the database and the user then goes through and tries to change the data that is under the lock, the process is going to end up ailing, and then they will see a communication come up that the object in question is not available for them to modify at this time. This helps you to make some of the changes in the system more permanent so as to avoid overwriting and other issues along the way.

Transforming the data using transactions is important because it allows the database to move from one state that was consistent with a new state that is consistent. There are times when you would want to do this, but it is critical to understand that the transactions can modify more than one kind of database at a time.

If you do end up going through and changing some of the data in the database that is a foreign key or a primary key without also updating this information in the other locations, this is going to create data that is seen as inconsistent, and then the SQL system is not going to accept what you are trying to do here.

Transactions are going to be a really big part of changing related data from multiple-table sources all at the same time. The transactional transformation is going to help keep the isolation in place, a property that prevents concurrent transactions from interfering with one another. If you are looking at the database, and you see that two transactions are happening at the same time, you will see that only one of these transactions is going to be successful.

The transactions that are happening are going to remain invisible and will remain that way until you are able to get them to complete fully. Whichever of the transactions is able to get done first, that will be the one that the system accepts. The new information displays when it is completed, and when the failed transactions are done in that way. When it gets to this point, the user is going to need to decide if the updated information is going to require the modifications or not.

If a power outage were to occur, and you find that the system stability is going to fail, then the data durability is going to step up and will make sure that the effects of an incomplete transaction are able to roll back to their original state. This may not end up exactly where you want it at the end of things, but at least you don't lose all of the work that you have done in this.

When you get to a point where one of the transactions is able to complete, but then another of the transactions doesn't end up finishing, then it is going to retain the completed transaction. Rollbacks are something that can be accomplished by a database engine using the log of transactions to identify the previous state of the data and then move the transactions back to this, ensuring that you don't lose out on all of the work that you have been doing.

Now, it is important to realize that there are going to be a few different variations of the database lock, and even various properties of locks at the same time. To start with are the lock properties, and these are going to include properties that include duration, granularity, and mode.

We will take a look at the duration, and the easiest way that we are able to define this term is that it is the way that specifies a time interval where the lock has been applied. The lock mode will define different types of locking, and these modes can be determined based on the type of resource being locked.

A shared lock can come into play with this as well, and this will allow the data reads while the row or page lock is in effect. Then there are exclusive locks that are going to be useful when you want to work with DML or data manipulation, and these locks are going to provide you with exclusive use of a page or a row for the execution of any modification that you would like to do. Exclusive locks are not going to take place in a concurrent manner, as data is going to be modified in an active manner; the page is then going to be inaccessible to all of the other users of the system, no matter their responsibilities or roles.

Then we can move to the update locks. These kinds of locks are going to be placed onto just one object, and this allows for the reading of the data while the lock is in place. It is also helpful because it will let the database determine whether or not an exclusive lock is necessary once you modify the transaction. The update lock is pretty much the best of both worlds, allowing the reading of data and DML transactions to happen at the same time at least until you are committing the actual update in the table or in the row.

This update lock is going to allow you to work on just the one option that you want, or the one part of the database, without affecting the use of all the others. Someone is not going to really be able to do much with that object, but they can still view it and see what is going on with it. Then, when it is all organized, and you are ready to work with the modification, the exclusive lock will be in place, just for as long as that modification took.

These types of locks are going to be known as page-level locking, but there are other options that you can use. We are just going to spend time on these ones because they are the ones that you are most likely to work with when you set up an SQL database.

The final property of a lock that we need to take a look at is the granularity which is going to specify to what degrees the resource is not going to be available. Rows are going to be the smallest object in the whole database that you are able to work with when you are doing manipulations. But the rows are not the only object type that you are able to work with when you do manipulations. Options like extents, tables, indices, and pages can be as well. And you also have a chance to lock up the entire database if you need to.

Before we move on here, we need to take a look at a process that is known as an extent. This is basically going to be the physical allocation of data, and the database engine is going to employ this lock if a table or an index grows, and more space on the disk is needed to hold onto it.

These can be used in some cases, but problems will come up when you use some of the locks, including a deadlock or a lock escalation, and it is important to be on the lookout for one of these. Before you start using the locks, it is best if you can get a full understanding of how these locks and how they work in the database so that you are able to use them in the proper manner.

The final chapter that we are going to take a look at in this guidebook is going to discuss some of the SQL administration, but it is useful before we get to this point to mention that Oracle was able to develop a few extensions for SQL, and one of these allows for procedural instruction using the SQL syntax. This extension is going to be known as PL/SL, and as we discussed a bit earlier, SL all on its own is not able to provide some of the procedural instructions that we need because it is going to be a non-procedural language.

The extension that is listed above is going to help fix this problem because it is responsible for extending out some of the capabilities that come with the SQL language. The PLSQL code is going to be used in many different manners, but for the most part, it is going to be used to help create and modify some of the more advanced concepts of SQL, such as the functions, stored procedures, and triggers.

Triggers are going to make it so that SL is able to perform specific operations as long as the conditional instructions have been defined with it. This means that when you do this, you are working with more advanced functionality of SQL, and this will often work at the same time with logging or alerts to notify both the principles and the administrators, depending on how you have this all set up when there are some errors in the database.

Remember here that the basic SQL code is not going to have the right kinds of control structures to do things like decision making, branching, and looping, which may be available in some of the coding languages including Java. Because of this, the PL/SQL was developed in order to meet the needs of the database product, which includes some of the functionality like the ones we talked about. Basically, this extension was developed to make sure that the SQL language was able to do some of the same functionalities that Java and other coding languages rely on as well. This ensures that you are able to get the most out of your SQL language when working in a database.

In addition, we also took a look at some of the topics of functions, we found that we talked a bit about functions that were user-defined, but we did not show how you were able to define them. This is another place where the SQL language does not adequately cover the creation of these kinds of functions. The good news is that when you use the right kind of program, you are able to create some functions that fit in well within the same scope as the system-defined functions that are accepted in SQL.

As a reminder, the user-defined function, or UDF, is going to be a construct of programming that is going to accept parameters, will perform tasks that can help the database use the parameters that the system defined, and will return the right results in a successful manner. These UDF's are going to be tricky in some cases because the SQL from Microsoft is going to allow for things that are known as stored procedures that are going to be able to accomplish the same task as these user-defined functions.

And finally, we need a quick word on the stored procedures. These are going to be a batch of statements in SQL that are going to be executed in more than one way, while also containing some centralized data access logic. Both of these features are going to be important when you work in SQL in production environments, but we won't go too much into this as it is above the beginner level for now.

Though we went into more details about some of the topics that we were able to talk about in this chapter, you will find that it helps to provide some great examples of how you are able to use SQL in the real world. There are so many companies and other entities that are going to rely on databases to help them keep track of the information that they need, whether this has to do with their employees or with their customers and even with their products.

There is a lot of information that a company is going to need to go through and keep track of overtime. And it is possible that they are going to have several different databases. The number of databases that a company has will depend on how big they are, but it is not uncommon to see them with a database for managing employees and employee work, one for customers, and one for any products that they end up selling.

Almost any company and industry will be able to work with these databases and see that it can benefit them. They can use it even if they provide more of a service to their customers rather than a lot of different products. But when you are storing information for your customers or for your employees, and you want to make sure that you are able to keep track of the products as well, then the topics we have been going through in this chapter, and with the rest of the guidebook, will be helpful for you.

There is so much that you can do when it comes to using a database in your business. And while there are many options to helping you get this database done, one of the best methods to go with is SQL. It is simple to use, doesn't take a lot of time to learn, and the coding is one of the easiest to learn out of all the programming languages.

Chapter 11: The Use of Database Administration

The last topic that we are going to look at here is the idea of database administration. Database administration, as well as database functionality, are going to be separate topics that all work on their own, but they are still very critical aspects that come with SL, and any base of knowledge is not going to be complete without having a chance to understand these related fields and how they relate to the SQL.

There are a lot of different administrative tasks that have to happen on a daily basis. Some of the most important ones that we need to talk about right now are going to include creating backups of the database the company is using, creating backups of the logs, and doing some performance management. In addition to this, there are going to be some other associated pieces of information that need to come into place including understanding how the storage of the database works, as well as the automation and the utilities of the database, but these are some areas of knowledge that will help them administrator become more effective, and won't really be involved in a direct manner in the maintenance of the database.

As we take a look at the SQL language, we can see that it contains some databases that are related to system information. These kinds of databases are going to provide some high-level information about the whole database system. This information is important because it is going to give the administrators at a glance data regarding the health and how well the performance of the database is doing.

The primary system database is what we are going to call the master database. Then when we look at the storage of the disk here, the basic unit for the storage is going to be known as "a page" or 8KB., and every database is only going to be one page in length, at least until the data contained inside of it is going to expand the database out to multiple pages. This can take some time depending on the size of your database and how quickly it ends up expanding out.

There are also going to be some utility functions that are going to exist inside of this language as well including bulk copy, which is going to allow the statements that you write out in this system to be entered into the command prompt.

Another part of administration on this language is going to be policy-based management. This will be based on the rules and the policies that are set up by a particular company and is customizable based on the company that is using it. This is basically a feature that is going to allow an administrator to control how the database is created and configured across all of the different user bases that are there. This is going to reinforce the data consistency, but can also make the job of the administrator a bit easier because they get to enforce the amount of consistency in how they maintain the database overall.

The database administrators, who are called DBA in SQL, will be responsible for creating the redundancy that is needed and to maximize the uptime on a database resource. They are able to do this because they assume and plan for the failure of the structures of the database. While no one wants the database to fail, they like to plan for this in case it does happen. The worst-case scenario with the database is that it would fail, but this is not something that the DBA should see as a possible outcome. This is going to cause a lot of problems with the system, could lose a lot of valuable information and this can cause more problems down the line.

Failure of the physical assets housing a database is a guarantee if enough time passes. The strain that can happen on the machine is high, and even under the steadiest of temperatures, there is a known limit on the number of re-writes that the physical dish is able to take on before the drive ends up failing. Redundancy is going to be created through housing data on some arrays that won't be able to come with data loss if you see that one of the nodes in the array fails. But there are other things that can cause failures in the system such as coding failures, power outages, and other things could cause some issues to the physical structure of that database if they are not taken care of in the proper manner.

The good news is that an experienced DBA is going to prepare and be ready in case any of these possibilities happen and most of them would be able to create some kind of solution that is automated so that, if failure happens (though they try to prevent it from ever happening), the least amount of data would be sacrificed as possible.

As our world of technology continues to grow and change, and we move more into the era of using cloud computing, the losses that are going to happen with failure will be pretty much nothing. But even when one of these companies doesn't decide to work with cloud computing, it is possible to do an automated backup of the database on a regular basis to make sure that the information is saved and ready to go.

If you are a DBA working with this kind of system, it is important to have something in place to handle the unexpected. You can prepare all that you want and try to avoid these problems as much as you can, but there is going to be times when things don't always go your way. Assuming that the worst is going to happen at any moment, and working with things like cloud computing if you can or at least having some backup that happens on a regular basis throughout the day, can ensure that if something happens the information from the database is saved and will do just fine when the system comes back up.

The next thing that we need to take a look at is how well the database is performing. This is something that the administration is going to need to deal with, but there are a lot of different factors that need to come into play with this one as well. Throughput and response times are the measurable that will help to quantify the performance. To start, the response time is going to measure a single operation from query to response, and throughput is able to help measure the overall ability to process transactions to the limit that the engine of the database is going to able to handle. There are three factors that we have to pay attention to if you are worried about the performance of the database, and these are going to include the available resources, the systems, and the database applications.

These three aspects are even able to be broken down into other things based on what you would like to look through and check out. This is because the system is going to have a lot of different parts. For example, when you are trying to work with the performance of your system, you need to look at things like how much memory is available, the speed of the CPU, the limitations on the system, the query optimization, and more. All of these factors are elaborated upon in previous chapters, which helps us to see more about what they are able to do and why they are so important to making this process work.

When we are looking at some of the more practice usages that come with this, the database system could contain a minimum of five hundred little databases, and each one is going to have their own coded statements, indices, and tables. The performance of the database is usually not going to be that big of a problem until the database has enough data that the speed of computing just isn't strong enough to override the efficiency.

This could be something that becomes a widespread situation in practice, and it is likely that many companies are going to rely on expert consultants to help deal with this kind of situation if it does arise in their company. This is because all of the offending factors are going to be so large in number, and in the case of doing SQL coding, it can be challenging to identify the full problem at hand.

With a good DBA, these problems should not be such a big deal, and you will be able to prevent them from happening in the first place. But when the DBA does not have the right experience to handle what is going on in the code, and they are not sure of the steps that they need to take to maintain and protect the database, it could result in some issues in the coding. This is when a professional is going to come in and can really help to fix the problems and will get the code to work the way that you need.

It is important to make sure that a competent DBA, and even a team of these individuals, will help you to manage your database and get it to work the way that you would like. This is an added expense for your business for sure, but the efficiency and the benefits that come with this will make the program work so much better than before.

The right DBA will be able to use the coding that comes with SQL to create and modify any of the tables and databases that you would like. They could take the customers or the employees who are able to use the database, and give those roles, allowing or restricting their access based on their role with the company and what they are allowed to see. If the CEO wants access to the database, they would have more than someone who is just working on one of the many projects in the database, for example. A customer would be limited to just being able to access their own account, rather than the account of anyone else who is on the system. This is one of the responsibilities that the DBA would be in charge of setting and monitoring.

In addition to keeping the database running well and making sure that no errors were going to come up, the DBA would need to work on the security that comes with the database. Those who are using the database expect that their information is going to be kept safe all of the time, and it would put a lot of people at risk, and harm the reputation of the company if they were not able to keep this information safe and secure for their customers and employees. This is why a DBA would need to spend some time and work, ensuring that the database is secure from all threats, internal and external, at all times.

Having a good DBA is going to make a big difference in how well the SQL database is going to work. They will be able to handle a lot of the different topics that we have discussed in this guidebook and will make sure that the database runs well and does what it should, with the help of the SQL coding language behind them.

Conclusion

Thank for making it through to the end of *SQL Programming*, let's hope it was informative and able to provide you with all of the tools you need to achieve your goals whatever they may be.

The next step is to start implementing some of the SQL languages into your business. There may be some other databases that you can use, and they may work with a lot of the different coding that you would need to do to keep information set and ready to go, but none are going to be as effective and helpful for helping you to manage your business as the SQL language.

This guidebook is going to help us learn more about the SQL language and some of the different things that you are able to with this database. This can help you to manage the data that you have, make it easier to pull up when it is needed, and so much more! No wonder so many businesses are running to use this kind of database to help them get results.

When you are ready to learn more about the SQL language and how to make it work for your needs, make sure to check out this guidebook and learn the steps that you need to make this process work for you.

Finally, if you found this book useful in any way, a review on Amazon is always appreciated!